Samuel French Acting Edition

Off Off Broadway Festival Plays, 44th Series

A Small Breach in Protocol at
Big Rick's Rockin' Skydive Academy
by Daniel Hirsch

Tidwell, or the Plantation Play
by Rodney Witherspoon II

Stay for Dinner
by Becky McLaughlin

Bunkmates
by Jeff Ronan

D1557225

Cluck Deluxe
by Bonnie Antosh

I Love You St. Petersburg!
by Bixby Elliot

SAMUELFRENCH.COM   SAMUELFRENCH.CO.UK

ISBN 978-0-573-70845-9

www.concordtheatricals.com
www.concordtheatricals.co.uk

FOR PRODUCTION ENQUIRIES

UNITED STATES AND CANADA
info@concordtheatricals.com
1-866-979-0447

UNITED KINGDOM AND EUROPE
licensing@concordtheatricals.co.uk
020-7054-7200

Each title is subject to availability from Concord Theatricals, depending
upon country of performance. Please be aware that *OFF OFF BROADWAY
FESTIVAL PLAYS, 44TH SERIES* may not be licensed by Concord
Theatricals in your territory. Professional and amateur producers should
contact the nearest Concord Theatricals office or licensing partner to verify
availability.

This work is published by Samuel French, an imprint of Concord Theatricals.

No one shall make any changes in this title(s) for the purpose of production. No part of this book may be reproduced, stored in a retrieval system, or transmitted in any form, by any means, now known or yet to be invented, including mechanical, electronic, photocopying, recording, videotaping, or otherwise, without the prior written permission of the publisher. No one shall upload this title(s), or part of this title(s), to any social media websites.

For all enquiries regarding motion picture, television, and other media rights, please contact Concord Theatricals.

MUSIC USE NOTE

Licensees are solely responsible for obtaining formal written permission from copyright owners to use copyrighted music in the performance of this play and are strongly cautioned to do so. If no such permission is obtained by the licensee, then the licensee must use only original music that the licensee owns and controls. Licensees are solely responsible and liable for all music clearances and shall indemnify the copyright owners of the play(s) and their licensing agent, Concord Theatricals, against any costs, expenses, losses and liabilities arising from the use of music by licensees. Please contact the appropriate music licensing authority in your territory for the rights to any incidental music.

IMPORTANT BILLING AND CREDIT REQUIREMENTS

If you have obtained performance rights to this title, please refer to your licensing agreement for important billing and credit requirements.

The Samuel French Off Off Broadway Short Play Festival (OOB) has been the nation's leading short play festival for forty-four years. The OOB Festival has served as a doorway to future success for aspiring writers. Over 200 plays have been published, and many participants have become established, award-winning playwrights.

For more information on the Samuel French Off Off Broadway Short Play Festival, including history, interviews, and more, please visit www.oobfestival.com.

Festival Sponsor: Concord Theatricals

Festival Artistic Director: Casey McLain
Literary Manager: Garrett Anderson
Blog Content Manager: Sarah Weber
Production Coordinators: Coryn Carson, Carly Erickson
Marketing Team: Sarah Kinsley Du, Jeremiah Hernandez, Courtney Kochuba, Imogen Lloyd Webber, Abbie Van Nostrand
Stage Manager: Kate Karczewski
House Manager: Tyler Mullen
Box Office Manager: Rosemary Bucher
Festival Staff: Garrett Anderson, Lissi Borschman, Jim Colleran, Samantha Cooper, Sean Demers, Sarah Kinsley Du, Zach Kaufer, Natty Koper, Fiona Kyle, Kayla Lambert, Nicole Matte, Alyssia McMorris, Alex Perez, Theresa Posorske, Becca Schlossberg, Rachel Smith, Alejandra Venancio

HONORARY GUEST PLAYWRIGHT

Lauren Yee

FESTIVAL JUDGES

Masi Asare
Eleanor Burgess
Clarence Coo
Vichet Chum
Chris Giordano
Keli Goff
David L. Kimple
Margaret Ledford
Emily Morse
Salem Tsegaye
Miriam Weiner
Alexis Williams

TABLE OF CONTENTS

FOREWORD

Samuel French is honored to have the six daring and inspirational playwrights included in this collection as the winners of our 44th Annual Off Off Broadway Short Play Festival. This year our Festival received over 800 submissions from around the world. We thank all of these gifted playwrights for sharing their talent with us and welcome each writer into our elite group of Off Off Broadway Festival winners.

We also wish to thank the producing companies who helped stage these works at our Festival. The vital relationship between playwright and theatre is one that we know well at Samuel French. Whether producing a Tony-winning play or developing a new work, theatre companies play a vital role in cultivating new audiences and communicating a playwright's vision. We commend them for this mission and thank each of the producers involved in the 44th Annual Festival for their tireless dedication and contributions to their playwright.

Perhaps the most challenging part of the OOB Festival is our production week. From our initial pool of Top-Thirty playwrights, we ultimately select six plays for publication and representation by Samuel French. Of course, we can't make our selections alone, so we enlist some brilliant minds within the theatre industry to help us in this process. Each night of the Festival, we have an esteemed group of three judges consisting of a Samuel French playwright and two other members of the theatre industry. We thank them for their support, insight, and commitment to the art of playwriting.

Samuel French is a 190-year-old company rich in history while at the same time dedicated to the future. We are constantly striving to develop groundbreaking methods that will better connect playwright and producer. With a team committed to continuing our tradition of publishing and licensing the best new theatrical works, we are boldly embracing our role in this industry as bridge between playwright and theatre.

On behalf of our board of directors; the entire Samuel French team in our New York, Los Angeles, and London offices; and the over 10,000 playwrights, composers, and lyricists that we publish and represent, we present you with the six winning plays of the 44th Annual Samuel French Off Off Broadway Short Play Festival.

This festival is about playwrights. Sharing the human story. We invite you to enjoy these extraordinary plays.

Casey McLain
Artistic Director
The Samuel French Off Off Broadway Short Play Festival

A Small Breach in Protocol at Big Rick's Rockin' Skydive Academy

Daniel Hirsch

A SMALL BREACH IN PROTOCOL AT BIG RICK'S ROCKIN' SKYDIVE ACADEMY was originally developed as part of PlayGround-LA's Monday Night PlayGround Series in Los Angeles in November 2018.

A SMALL BREACH IN PROTOCOL AT BIG RICK'S ROCKIN' SKYDIVE ACADEMY was produced as part of MeetCute Los Angeles at Thymele Arts on May 2, 2019. The production was directed by Annie McVey. The cast was as follows:

RAE	Geri-Nikole Love
ALICIA	Kari Nicolle
TINA	Kay Wilson
CHAD	Andy Dubick

A SMALL BREACH IN PROTOCOL AT BIG RICK'S ROCKIN' SKYDIVE ACADEMY was produced as part of the 44th Annual Samuel French Off Off Broadway Short Play Festival at the Vineyard Theatre in New York City on August 23, 2019. The production was directed by Stephen M. Eckert. The cast was as follows:

RAE	Rachel Yong
ALICIA	Hannah Mitchell
TINA	Eleanor Pearson
CHAD	Henry Ayres-Brown

CHARACTERS

RAE – (thirties/forties, f) introverted, serious, not prone to risk-taking

ALICIA – (thirties/forties, f) tenderhearted Type A, extremely not prone to risk-taking

TINA – (twenties/thirties, f) highly competent skydiving instructor, this is her Tuesday

CHAD – (twenties/thirties, m) rookie skydiving instructor, a sweetheart, totally pumped to be here

SETTING

A tiny, old airplane; mid-air; a landing field

TIME

Late afternoon

AUTHOR'S NOTE

A slash (/) indicates a moment of interrupted speech.

(A tiny, old airplane that is very loud.)

*(On parallel bench seats, **RAE** is strapped in tandem to **CHAD**, and **ALICIA** is strapped in tandem to **TINA**. They are all in skydiving gear.)*

*(**RAE** looks terrified. **ALICIA** looks concerned.)*

ALICIA. *(Shouting.)* It's not too late!

RAE. What?

ALICIA. It's not too late...to change your mind about this. *(To **TINA**.)* We can do that, right?

TINA. It's going to be great!
*(To **CHAD**.)* Altitude check.

CHAD. About a thousand from the exit.

RAE. *(To **ALICIA**.)* What did you say?
*(To **CHAD**.)* We can't just stay in the plane, can we?

CHAD. You stoked?!

ALICIA. I said it's not too late to change your mind!
*(To **TINA**.)* We can still change our minds, right? We don't normally do things like this. But she insisted and I told her going skydiving on a Groupon may not be totally fucking / prudent but she insisted.

TINA. *(To **ALICIA**.)* Open your arms when you fall. Out not up. Like a flying squirrel.

CHAD. *(To **RAE**.)* Smile!

*(He holds up a GoPro. **RAE** smiles weakly.)*

ALICIA. *(To **TINA**.)* How long / have you been doing this?

TINA. We'll be falling for about sixty seconds.

ALICIA. That's not / what I –

RAE. *(To **ALICIA**.)* I need to do this.

TINA. *(To **CHAD**.)* You check the routing on your bridle?

ALICIA. *(To* **RAE.***)* What did you say?

RAE. I've got to do this.

> *(***CHAD** *checks gear and gives* **TINA** *a thumbs-up.)*

ALICIA. Rae, are you okay?

CHAD. Almost there!

CHAD & TINA. Let's go Big Rick's Rockin' Skydive Academy!

RAE. *(Quietly.)* No. I'm not okay. I'm not okay.

ALICIA. *(To* **TINA.***)* She insisted we do this and I don't know why. This is / completely terrifying!

TINA. *(To* **CHAD.***)* What about the pin on your pilot chute?

RAE. *(Quietly.)* I'm not okay.

ALICIA.	**CHAD.**
(To **RAE.***)* What?	*(To* **TINA.***)* What?

ALICIA. Rae, what did you say?

TINA. The pilot chute?! The pin! Chad!

> *(***CHAD** *grins into the GoPro.)*

CHAD. We have achieved altitude!

TINA.	**ALICIA.**
Chad!	RAE!

CHAD. Wooooohoooo!

> *(***CHAD** *with* **RAE** *pushes up off the bench. They are now falling through space out of the airplane.)*
>
> *(***TINA** *with* **ALICIA** *pushes up off the bench. They too are now falling through space out of the airplane.)*
>
> *(A shift. Time slows down. The following dialogue is the rush of thoughts.)*
>
> *(***TINA** *and* **CHAD** *check altimeters strapped to their wrists to determine altitude as they fall.)*

ALICIA. Oh no. Oh no. Oh no.

Oh.

Oh.

Acceleration. Force.

Whooooooa.

Blood. God.

Rush rush rush.

The air, viscous, thick. An unstoppable current of air.
Skin feels electric.

Ahhhhhhhh.

TINA. 9,000 feet until parachute deployment.

Fucking Chad. He didn't do what I asked him to do.

CHAD. 8,900 feet until I pull the cord.

What was Tina trying to tell me back in the plane?

RAE. Air. So much air.

Air. Air. Air. Air. Air. Air. Air.

Lump in my gut. I feel it grow.

I'm going to die. I'm going to die. I'm going to die.

TINA. 8,700 feet.

He didn't check the pilot chute. And you always have to
check the pin. That's protocol.

CHAD. 8,300 feet.

Huh, did I check the...? Oh...

ALICIA. Oh my god.

This is.

It.

We're in it now.

Whoa.

Flying through heaven.

Swimming in rivers of atmosphere.

Touching the divine.

Holy shit.

Wall of air.

Force of wind.

Speed.

Yes, speed.

Speed. Speed. Speed. Speed. Speed. Speed.

Did I just, did I just...cum?

Open my arms.

And I am a fucking bird.

TINA. 7,900 feet.

This is all my fault.

7,200 feet.

I told Big Rick Chad was ready. Chad is clearly not ready.

6,400 feet.

Please be okay, Chad. I need you to be okay.

CHAD. 5,400 feet.

OH. SHIT.

4,300 feet.

RAE. Speed and air and wind and force

and

and

Lump in my gut.

And then there is this:

I still haven't told her yet.

I got the phone call from the doctor three weeks ago.

I go in for another biopsy next week.

Why haven't I told her yet?

Look at the earth.

Look at the earth.

I'm going to die.

TINA. 3,200 feet.

As a Big Rick's Rockin' Skydive Academy employee I have made over 3,000 jumps.

3,000 feet.

A fatal mistake was inevitable in one of them.

CHAD. 2,000 feet.

Oh no no no no no no no no no no no no no no no no no.

ALICIA. Atmosphere wraps around me.

Lungs expand, heart floods, blood quickens.

I am in love with the world. Love. Love. Love.

Letting go is falling in love.

Letting go is finally knowing your life is bigger than you ever realized.

Letting go is having power.

I am a fucking bird!

TINA. 1,500 feet.

It's out of my hands now.

1,400 feet.

I'm sorry. I'm so sorry.

CHAD. 1,300 feet.

There's no freaking way to know if the pilot chute is functioning now.

1,200 feet.

I'm sorry Tina. You believed in me. Maybe even cared about me?

1,100 feet.

I'm sorry I screw everything up.

1,000 feet.

I'm sorry chick strapped to me whose name I forgot.

900 feet.

I'm sorry Mom.

800 feet.

I'm sorry Big Rick!

RAE. Every minute of my life.

Look at the earth.

Cow fields. Suburban forest. Highway curlicues. Mountains in distant haze.

My job. My apartment. My wife. My lump of cells in my gut.

How much is left?

How many times...

How many more times will I hold Alicia in my arms?

I'm going to die.

I'm going to die.

I'm going to die.

But then there is this:

> *(Something in the atmosphere changes.* **RAE** *laughs.)*

But...

Maybe?

Fuck!

Who knows?!

There's no way to know, really. There's no way. No way.

Up here, horizons of possibility expand.

Up here, it's like the cancer doesn't exist.

Maybe I left it somewhere behind in the stratosphere.

Evaporated in the force of wind.

Maybe, maybe, maybe.

I'm so glad we did this.

TINA. 500 feet until chute deployment.

CHAD. 100 feet until I pull the cord.

ALICIA. Feel the air. I am a bullet.

I am a rocket.

I am a God.

I am an unstoppable force.

And I don't feel afraid.

Why would I ever feel that way again?

I am a fucking bird.

TINA. Fifty feet.

CHAD. Ten feet.

ALICIA. THIS.

CHAD & TINA. Zero feet.

RAE. LIFE!

TINA. PLEASE!

(She pulls her cord. A whoosh of air. **TINA** *and* **ALICIA** *are pulled back by the drag of their parachutes.)*

CHAD. I pull the cord. I see what happens. I hope.

(He pulls his cord. Nothing happens. He pulls his cord a second time.)

(Finally, a whoosh of air. **CHAD** *and* **RAE** *are pulled back by a functioning parachute.)*

(A shift. Time resumes at its regular pace. They speak to one another.)

YEEEEEEHAAAAAW! WOOOHOOOO!!

*(***TINA** *looks over and sees* **CHAD** *[with* **RAE***] floating in the air near her [with* **ALICIA***].)*

TINA. Oh thank God.

ALICIA. I know, right?!

TINA. You have a good fall?

ALICIA. It was amazing.

CHAD. *(To* **RAE.***)* You doing okay...buddy?

RAE. *(To* **CHAD.***)* Yeah. I'm okay. I'm going to be okay.

CHAD. Nice view, right?

RAE. Incredible.

TINA. *(To* **ALICIA.***)* Now we just drift down to Earth.

CHAD. *(To* **RAE.***)* Now we just drift down to Earth.

(A moment of quiet as they all drift.)

(Impact.)

*(***TINA** *unstraps from* **ALICIA.** **CHAD** *unstraps from* **RAE.***)*

ALICIA. Ahhh! Yes! That was... Gahhhh!

RAE. I can't believe we...! Oh my God!

*(***ALICIA** *runs to* **RAE** *and hugs her.)*

*(***TINA** *runs to* **CHAD,** *hugs him, then immediately pushes him down to the ground.)*

TINA. *(Quietly.)* You need to check the pin and the bridle and the pilot chute every single time, okay?! It's Big Rick's Rockin' Skydive Academy protocol. Protocol saves lives.

(**CHAD** *looks like he's going to cry.*)

CHAD. I know. I know. I'm... I know.

TINA. It's okay. Let's just gather the chutes.

CHAD. Tina, I'm so, so sorry.

TINA. *(Eyeing their charges.)* Hey, hey. Shut up. It's fine. Everybody's fine.
(Pulling **CHAD** *away.)* I'm really, really glad you're okay. Like really glad.

CHAD. Me too.

(**TINA** *and* **CHAD** *move off, busy with cleanup work.*)

ALICIA. I can't even...
Wasn't that...?
I've never felt anything like that before.
I mean... Damn.
I am a fucking bird.

RAE. Good. That's great, honey.

ALICIA. It was. It is. I feel like I'm invincible. Like suddenly... I can do anything. Take on anything. Like fuck being scared. You know?

RAE. Good.

(*They hug again.* **ALICIA** *gives* **RAE** *a kiss.*)

ALICIA. I didn't think this was something you would ever want to do. Frankly, you're not that kind of girl. Hell, I'm not that kind of girl either. And I didn't get why you were so insistent that we do this, but fuck.
I'm glad we did.

(**RAE** *nods. She is, too.*)

You hungry? I'm starving. I could eat my weight in mozzarella sticks.

RAE. Mozzarella sticks?

ALICIA. I know, right? I just have a very specific craving. And I mean, we're young and healthy, we deserve fried cheese.

RAE. ...

ALICIA. We can also not eat mozzarella sticks if you're not into it.

RAE. No. That sounds great.

> ...

> The thing is... I was thinking...we have no idea what's going to happen. Like anything could happen to either one of us at any moment and... I mean, we have no idea.

ALICIA. Sure, yeah...what are you talking about?

RAE. I just... Let's keep doing stuff like this? Let's keep living a life filled with things like this no matter what happens. Because we never know what comes next, you know?

ALICIA. What's going to happen, Rae?

RAE. ...

ALICIA. Hey. No matter what happens, I'm in. If we jump out of planes, if we eat mozzarella sticks or we don't eat mozzarella sticks – though my craving is pretty intense right now and they'll be delicious. If you get hit by a bus and your face gets torn off, if you get old and sick or old and boring, I'm here. I'm not afraid of anything anymore. I'm a fucking bird, okay?

RAE. Okay.

ALICIA. Let's go stuff our faces before it gets too late?

RAE. Okay.

> (**ALICIA** *grabs* **RAE**'s *hands. They walk off.*)

Tidwell, or the Plantation Play

Rodney Witherspoon II

TIDWELL, OR THE PLANTATION PLAY was first presented at the Brown University/Trinity Repertory Company MFA Program's First Look Festival on January 14, 2019 in Providence, Rhode Island. The production was directed by Jessica Natalie Smith. The cast was as follows:

ACTOR 1 . . . . Lizzy Brooks
ACTOR 2 . . . . Christopher Lindsay
SAL . . . . Gunnar Manchester
TAMMY . . . . .Madeleine Barker
ZACHARY . . . . Andrew Gombas

TIDWELL, OR THE PLANTATION PLAY was produced as part of the 44th Annual Samuel French Off Off Broadway Short Play Festival at the Vineyard Theatre in New York City on August 22, 2019. The production was directed by Kimille Howard. The cast was as follows:

ACTOR 1 . . . . Jessica Natalie Smith
ACTOR 2 . . . . Rodney Witherspoon II
SAL . . . . .Ben Schrager
TAMMY . . . . .Caitlin Brzezinski
ZACHARY . . . . Keith Weiss

CHARACTERS

ACTOR 1 – Black woman, twenties/thirties

ACTOR 2 – Black man, twenties/thirties

SAL – White man, visibly older than Tammy, his wife

TAMMY – White woman, visibly younger than Sal, her husband

ZACHARY – White man, teen, Tammy's son and Sal's stepson; a guerrilla filmmaker

SETTING

A slave quarter

TIME

Summer, Present Day

I think it wiser...not to keep the sores of war but to follow the examples of those nations who endeavored to obliterate the marks of civil strife, to commit to oblivion the feelings engendered.

– Robert E. Lee (1869)

(SETTING: An "intimate" slave cabin. It leaks from the roof. Minimal setting, as with any slave quarters. A window. A small cot. A bucket and washboard. A few stools. A fireplace with hanging cast-iron pots. A couple of other buckets around the room.)

*(AT RISE: In the dark, **ACTOR 1** is humming. After some time, a cell phone screen flashes. A text message is received. As the phone screen lights up, a face can be seen. She is laughing at the texts. The phone is buzzing, maybe a sound. More laughter with each message.)*

(Lights up. We see her in a long, worn, floor-length dress, her only dress, pregnant. Hair in braids, somewhat clean braids – edges are for the most part in place. She's still focused on the phone.)

ACTOR 1. *(Speaking her message as she types.)* Uh – uh...tell her...she needs to...get her ass...out of...her feelings... and have...some...dranks...with us.

> *(She sends the message. Waits. A message is received. She laughs.)*

> *(**ACTOR 2** enters, slightly wet. His clothing worn, shoes beaten, satchel weathered.)*

ACTOR 2. I hate being wet.

ACTOR 1. Don't go outside then.

ACTOR 2. I needed to smoke real quick.

ACTOR 1. Couldn't you have waited? It's almost time. Fifteen minutes.

ACTOR 2. Thank God.

> *(Beat.)*

ACTOR 2.   **ACTOR 1.**
 (Checks pocket watch.) 4:46!   *(Checks phone.)* 4:46!

ACTOR 2. I'm gonna quit. I feel it coming.

ACTOR 1. Quit smoking in the rain?

ACTOR 2. Naw, girl. Look at this.

   (Points to leaking roof.)

What are these working conditions? And the schedule? It's stupid. Look at me. I'm in these busted leather shoes all day. My toes literally wink at me with every step I take. No comfortable shoes, at all?

ACTOR 1. Wanna get drinks with us?

ACTOR 2. I'll pass.

ACTOR 1. You never go out with us. You must hate us.

ACTOR 2. Okay. Say that I do go. What are we going to talk about? Our favorite cotton-picking hymns? Or the kid that threw up during the whipping last week?

ACTOR 1. The kid had a visceral response. I would've done the same.

ACTOR 2. I am classically trained – and so are you!

ACTOR 1. Summer stock didn't want us. We're broke.

   (Looks at phone.)

Aye, 4:47!

ACTOR 2. We have master's degrees, for Christ's sake. You have a theater company.

ACTOR 1. *(Teasingly.)* You signed the contract. You thought you'd be different.

ACTOR 2. I thought that *it* would be different. Sure, they gave us the freedom to rewrite the story and make it our own –

ACTOR 1. Still a slave story.

ACTOR 2. What?

ACTOR 1. No matter the contract signed or intentions behind a new narrative, you're still on this plantation. Singing and "picking cotton" on some days, but mostly spending the day with baby momma and her bun in the oven.

(She slaps around the fake belly in her dress. More teasing.)

You signed up for this.

(Beat.)

ACTOR 2. Yeah. I thought that *I* would be different.

(Thunder crashes. Rain showers the tin rooftop. Water begins to drip into the room. Lightning. Through the window, we see **SAL**, **TAMMY**, *and* **ZACHARY** *standing. Maybe silhouettes. The* **ACTORS** *do not notice. Thunder crashes again. Rain pours. Lightning. No one is outside of the window.)*

I hate this place! I swear, I am leaving this week.

ACTOR 1. We have four weeks left. If you leave now, you'll forfeit your final payment and –

(A phone notification.)

Hold on. It's Tracy.

(She reads.)

Patrons...on premises...looking to be...walking in your...direction.

ACTOR 2. Aw fuck.

ACTOR 1. Forreal?! The shift is almost done. The big house is playing games. This place wasn't built to comfortably shelter a group of bodies. Not today!

(Lifts her dress to retrieve a radio strapped to her waist. We see that she is wearing colorful, vibrant leggings and UGG boots underneath, but all of these are not visible when standing.)

(Into the radio.) Quarter Five to big house.

(Silence from radio.)

Big house, do you copy?

ACTOR 2. That's the shit I'm talking about. Doesn't the plantation close in like ten minutes? We are definitely stationed in the middle of the tour route.

ACTOR 1. Some nerve.

ACTOR 2. Fuck leaving "this week." Today might have to be my last shift, sis.

>   *(The door swings open. No one enters. Beat.)*

ACTOR 1. Hello?

>   *(Beat. The* **FAMILY** *bursts into the room, slightly wet. The* **ACTORS** *jump in shock, then regain composure. The guests roam the space, toward the fire.)*

>   *(To the group, stepping out of their ways.)* Um, okay... hello y'all.

SAL.	ZACHARY.	TAMMY.
Hey!	*(Eyes glued to phone.)* I've said it before and I'll say it again, this place is weird.	Well hello!

>   *(Awkward silence.)*

ACTOR 1. Just make yourselves at, uh, home. There's not much space here, but it's what we have to work with.

ZACHARY. My room is bigger than this –

TAMMY. Well count your blessings, hun. This is a shack for slaves –

SAL. It has a special charm.

ZACHARY. Even at the hotel. My hotel room is bigger than this.

SAL. I hope that we aren't of any inconvenience. The sun was shining so bright earlier.

ACTOR 2. There's an app for that, but okay.

TAMMY. *(To* **ACTOR 1**.*)* Well, the weather channel did mention something like this.

ACTOR 1. Oh, we completely understand.

TAMMY. We could have saved this trip for *any* other day this summer, but Sal was so insistent. He had to come today. And when Sal wants something, he gets it –

SAL. Tammy, now, don't put this all on me. Let's not forget that *you* scheduled the flight out for right after the closing ceremony of the reunion. You knew I had to see the plantation before leaving.

ACTOR 1. So...you guys are from around here?

SAL. One could say that we are the *true* natives of this land.

ACTOR 2. *(To* **ACTOR 1.***)* Interesting! –

ACTOR 1. Well, it's nice to have you...back. The rain shouldn't last for long. If you need anything, let us know.

> *(She turns away to apply makeup and clean up her hairstyle, as if preparing to leave. Maybe even stripping down from her costume to hang it up.)*

ACTOR 2. We just need to reset a few props and furniture in here. Don't mind us.

TAMMY. This would be the perfect time for these here hoagies I slaved over.

> *(To* **ZACHARY.***)* Hey you! Put the phone down. Come eat.

SAL. Oh no! Are you closing down so soon?

> *(The* **ACTORS** *share a look.)*

ACTOR 1. This is usually the time that we start to wrap things up in our quarters.

SAL. But the plantation closes at five.

ACTOR 2. Yes. And it's 4:50.

SAL. I know.

> *(Long pause.)*

ACTOR 2. We never have guests here around this time. The big house doesn't admit new groups beyond 4:30.

SAL. Well...they had no problem letting us in. We're here now.

> *(Beat.)*

TAMMY. We are so sorry to be in your way. Carry on with –

SAL. Now now, Tam Tam. We trekked this whole way to get here. Can't we at least enjoy the show that we paid for?

ZACHARY. *(To the* **ACTORS.***)* I really didn't want to be here. It's weird here –

SAL. Tam, I'm sure the slaves wouldn't mind doing their bit for us. It's only a few minutes. And this is Zachary's first time here. I told you that some family history could benefit him. And it is raining. Some entertainment could help pass the time.

ZACHARY. *(Into phone.)* Not really my family history. I'm entertained. I'm all right –

TAMMY. *(To ZACHARY.)* Well your father and I aren't always in our phones, now aren't we?

> *(Beat.)*

ACTOR 1. *(To ACTOR 2.)* It wouldn't kill us to perform the piece. It's only a few minutes long.

ACTOR 2. *(Under breath.)* Shit, I'm leaving at five, rain or shine –

SAL. What was that?

ACTOR 2. *(Grinning.)* I'd love to. Rain or shine, the show must go on.

SAL. Fantastic! See?

TAMMY. Oh goodie!

> *(To ZACHARY.)* Get over here boy and put that phone down. Now, I didn't pay five dollars for your ticket for you to text –

ACTOR 2. *(To ACTOR 1.)* Five dollars?!

ACTOR 1. Are you subscribers?

SAL. We're lifetime subscribers. Whether we come often or not, the Tidwell Plantation will always have our support.

TAMMY. We visit *maybe* once a year, God willing. We're members at the "Sweet Tea" level.

SAL. We used to be at the "King Cotton" level, but we had to cut back a few things.

ACTOR 1. Just give us a moment to prepare. And please leave this area of the floor open. So feel free to sit on the bed and the chairs –

ACTOR 2. So, we're really doing this?

ACTOR 1. They're *members*. I'm sure this would be a good look for us considering the circumstances.

ACTOR 2. *(Whispered.)* Whatever.

TAMMY. Oh goodie!

(To **ZACHARY.***)* Hey you, off the phone.

> *(***ACTOR 2*** exits the room.* **ACTOR 1** *sets her position inside. Stage goes dark. In the dark, a hymn is brewing. The fire burns.* **ACTOR 1** *is at the pot at the fire, stirring. She sings "Swing Low, Sweet Chariot." Lights fade in. She sings with a pain in her voice. Maybe turns away to do some minor task, but always returning to the stove.)*

SAL. *(Whispered.)* Oh I love this hymn! I bought the CD at the gift shop last year.

> *(***ACTOR 1*** does react to the comments, but remains composed. Continues singing. After some time,* **ACTOR 2** *enters. Pours out some items from the satchel on the twin-sized cot; some lingering cotton falls out in the pour. He is even more wet. He embraces* **ACTOR 1** *and joins in the song.)*

TAMMY. Oh my word. They are better than last year's slaves.

> *(***ACTOR 2*** tries to hold back a response. He moves over to the washboard. After some time, the song ends on a peaceful, harmonized note.* **ACTOR 1** *returns to cooking.* **ACTOR 2** *begins work at the washboard.)*

ACTOR 1. You better bring the clothesline in here. A storm looks to be rollin' in.

ACTOR 2. Mhm.

> *(He exits and returns with clothes and line.)*

Watcha fixin' over there?

ACTOR 1. Makin' somethin' I know you gon' like.

ACTOR 2. Collards?

ACTOR 1. Well –

ACTOR 2. Chicken stew?!

ACTOR 1. Boy, quit while you're ahead.

ACTOR 2. Hope it's good, Ma, I'm starving.

>*(Thunder crashes. Rain showers the tin rooftop. Water begins to drip into the room in another area.)*

(Annoyed by the leak, finds another bucket.) We gotta leave this place.

ACTOR 1. What?

ACTOR 2. We need to go. I can't stay here any longer. The spirit is moving me –

ACTOR 1. What are you talkin' about –

ACTOR 2. You wanna stay here the rest of your life? Die here, like the rest of 'em –

ACTOR 1.	**ACTOR 2**.
Where? Where are you goin'? And this baby –	Yo' mamma, paw, my brotha – *We* are goin'. Somewhere far.

ACTOR 2. The baby too. What, you think I'm leavin' you and the baby? We all have to go.

>*(He embraces **ACTOR 1**.)*

We can't stay here. I can't raise a baby here. I don't wanna go through that again –

ACTOR 1. Where, where?

>*(Sounds of horse and carriage from a distance.)*

ACTOR 2. North. It's a long travel from what they say. We might die on the way...but it's better than being here –

ACTOR 1. Shhh, someone is comin'.

>*(Lights fade out as they hold each other. Beat.)*

SAL. *(Whispered.)* I don't remember that part.

>*(Lights up.)*

TAMMY.	**ZACHARY.**	**SAL.**
(Wildly clapping, almost in tears.) Wonderful! Oh my, just – and the baby – and the singing was just – yes!	*(Genuinely interested.)* Wow. I can't – That was lit.	*(Confused.)* I don't remember that, any of that from last time.

ACTOR 1. Thank you!

ACTOR 2. Yes, thank you, thank you!

    (To **ACTOR 1.***)* All right. I'm outta here. I'm done.

ACTOR 1. But it's still raining –

SAL. *(Approaching.)* I have a few questions.

    (Short pause.)

ACTOR 2. Um, let me just change this shirt first.

ACTOR 1. What would you like to know?

SAL. So – well, first, great performance. I liked the singing and ambiance. Great shack, accurate design. Though... my only qualm –

ACTOR 2. Qualm –

SAL. Is with the storyline.

ACTOR 2. What about it?

SAL. Typically, uh, now, I've been coming here for a few years –

TAMMY. Decades –

SAL. Yes, decades, and usually, well, it typically goes something like this –

    (He proceeds to loosely recreate the blocking.)

So, it starts with her cooking, of course. Pregnant and all, singing and such. And then he enters – also those shoes aren't of the period.

ACTOR 1. Oh, yes, uh, it's just I'm on my feet all day and the dress is long enough to hide my feet. I really don't walk away from this cooking bit for the whole scene –

SAL. It's not period and she's typically barefoot. Anyways, he enters, the satchel and cotton on the bed, hugs her, sings, yada yada yada.

TAMMY. He's such a stickler for details.

SAL. So then he goes on to the washboard and does the clothes business. THEN – this is where it's different – he tells her about all the gossip. You know, the plans for the next Sunday revival –

ACTOR 1. *(Bewildered.)* O...kay –

SAL. And how Coffey and Barnaby are no longer at the Morgan plantation. They tried to run away and, well, you know what happens to runaways.

ACTOR 2. *(Overly sarcastic.)* No I don't. Do tell me.

ZACHARY. *(To* **ACTOR 1.***)* Haha. I like him.

SAL. They were captured and hanged by some nearby overseers.

ACTOR 2. Of course.

SAL. So, he tells her all of this and she proceeds to tell him about what she's going to cook for the revival and make that thing that Coffey used to like, in her memory. Then he goes on to talk about how they will never do what Coffey and Barnaby did because they are so blessed to have the Tidwells and they treat them well. And then it ends with them embracing each other and envisioning bringing in this new child into such a beautiful world. And then it ends.

ZACHARY. *(To* **ACTOR 1**, *embarrassed.)* Please excuse them. They're embarrassing. They weren't trained in cultural sensitivity.

TAMMY. Oh, and the field. The field is so lush. Just a sea of white rustling in the breeze. But, of course, we aren't going to see that today, now are we?

SAL. Do they still sing in the field, that mellifluous hymn? What was it? "Go Down Moses"?

ACTOR 1. Yeah.

SAL. *(To* **TAMMY.***)* Ooooh, that's my favorite! Track number eight. We'll listen to it on the way to the airport. Louis Armstrong sings it so well.

TAMMY. Remember our second date? Sal brought me here on our second date a few years ago. We had our first kiss to track number eight.

ZACHARY. *(To* **ACTOR 1.***)* Oddly, I am here for all of this nonsense.

SAL. Everything here has been the same for years –

TAMMY. Decades.

> *(Looking through her bag, talking to no one in particular. She begins to enter another world. Think* Food Network *show presentational.)*

Oh, and I also made a Kwanzaa cake. I thought I'd make it for you people. A token of appreciation for the work you do here.

ACTOR 2. Kwanzaa...cake?

ZACHARY. *(Whispers to* **ACTOR 2.***)* Psst. Don't eat it. It's terrible.

SAL. It just isn't right to change things around here. Did they let you change the story?

TAMMY. It's so delicious –

ACTOR 1. Who is "they"?

TAMMY. *(Pulls cake out of bag.)* It's an angel food cake –

SAL. The directors of plantation entertainment.

TAMMY.	**ACTOR 2.**
With vanilla frosting and a lil cocoa powder for that rich brown color –	Ha! No. We saw the script, were dissatisfied, and rewrote it. It didn't feel right.

SAL. Well, *your* little story was not right. The original was quaint and wholesome.

TAMMY. Apple filling in the middle –

ACTOR 1. And ours was…?

TAMMY.	**SAL**.
Topped with corn nuts, pumpkin seeds, and popcorn –	Defiant. It was defiant.

ACTOR 2. Lynching is peaceful and wholesome?

TAMMY. I even have the Kwanzaa candles to stick in it and light. See? Just give me one – *(Digs in bag for candles.)*

SAL. Well, not that part. But the plantation was such a peaceful, picturesque place. No need to tamper with that model.

TAMMY. Here they are!

> *(She whips the candles out of her bag, sticks each candle in the cake. Lights as she explains.)*

Seven candles for seven days. This one is for Umoja, which in African means "unity."

ACTOR 1. I'm over this conversation.

TAMMY. This one here is Kuji… Kuji…chakalaka, which means like "family matters"…or "good times"…or something –

SAL. If he would have left those landowners and slaves alone, we'd be livin' peaceful lives, on acres of land, much like this –

ACTOR 2. Why? Why do you care so damn much?

SAL. *(Frantic.)* Because this is my heritage. We existed here and had power here and I'm not losing that power. My family fought to save this land.

ACTOR 2. Who was working this land?

SAL. My whole family…and some additional help – do you know how expensive a slave was?

ZACHARY. *(Texting but still present.)* Nope. Don't want to know. Don't need to know. Stop while you're ahead.

TAMMY.	ACTOR 1.
(At this point, six candles are lit, with one left.) And this baby here is Imani, which means "keep hope alive" –	*(Under her breath.)* Can someone please shut this lady up!

ACTOR 2. Don't romanticize slavery!

TAMMY. Let's all take a break here and have a slice of –

ACTOR 1. *(Slow burn fury. Finally addressing* **TAMMY** *head-on.)* Nobody...wants...A SLICE...OF YOUR FUCKING FILTHY KWANZAA CAKE. So, you and your husband and your privileged son can take this appropriation pastry and shove it up YOUR ASSES! And Kwanzaa is in the winter. IT'S JULY DAMMIT! I can't believe this.

> *(A Silence.* **TAMMY** *is choked up and swelling inside.* **ZACHARY** *is grinning.)*

What the hell is a Kwanzaa cake?!

TAMMY. *(Shaking.)* I just... I just wanted to –

SAL. How dare you? Years ago, your people would never have the types of mouths that you have.

ACTOR 1. Yeah? This is not "years ago." This plantation is just for show. I would burn this bitch down with you all in it if I had nothing to lose.

> *(***TAMMY***, stunned, runs out of the room in tears. After a moment,* **ZACHARY** *runs after her. A standoff between the* **ACTORS** *and* **SAL.***)*

SAL. How dare you?

ACTOR 1. Oh, what are you going to do? Hang me out for the world to see? I'm not Coffey.

> *(Beat.)*

Try me.

SAL. If I could –

> *(He turns to see* **ACTOR 2** *in the line of the door. He is stuck between the two.)*

SAL. My family fought for this country, for this land. You people have no respect.

ACTOR 2. You don't want any problems with us. Believe me.

ACTOR 1. Don't let the illusion fool you, Tidwell. We are not your property.

SAL. How dare you? I can't wait to tell them all about you.

ACTOR 1. Tell all of your friends until you are blue in the face.

ZACHARY. *(Enters.)* Let's go Sal. You're done here. It's all over. *(Leading* **SAL** *out the door.)*
(With a smile, to the **ACTORS**.*)* Thank you both.

> *(He shoves* **SAL** *out the door.)*

> *(Shakes the* **ACTORS**' *hands.)*

For everything. This was all...insightful.

> *(Laughs. Exits. Shuts the door. The* **ACTORS** *are clearly exhausted.)*

ACTOR 1. I never want to see that man again.

ACTOR 2. I bet you don't. The only thing worse than being on a plantation is not having the option to leave.

ACTOR 1. I'm done with this place.

> *(Blackout.)*

Stay for Dinner

Becky McLaughlin

STAY FOR DINNER was first produced by Spirit Gum Theatre Company as part of the 44th Annual Samuel French Off Off Broadway Short Play Festival at the Vineyard Theatre in New York City on August 22, 2019. The performance was directed by Sally Meehan, with costumes by Sarah Jenkins, makeup by Caitlin Stafford, and props by Becky McLaughlin. The cast was as follows:

JOE	Michael Ackerman
JENNY	Caitlin Stafford
GIRL #1 / GIRL #4 (CHLOE)	Rachel Hundert
BOY #1 / BOY #3 / BOY #6	Sean Riehm
GIRL #2 / GIRL #7	Beth Devlin
"GIRL" #3 / BOY #2 / BOY #5	Jon Furr
GIRL #5 / GIRL #6	Sarah Jenkins
BOY #4 / BOY #7	Brad Heikes

CHARACTERS

JOE – a boy in his late teens/early twenties
JENNY – a girl in her late teens/early twenties

HAUNTED HOUSE VISITORS

(Range from six to fourteen actors who can repeat or be cast individually. An ethnic identity or age is not specifically required for any part, and gender can also be assigned as preferred. Suggested casting below to minimize the number of actors needed.)

GIRL #1 / GIRL #4 (CHLOE)
GIRL #2
GIRL #3 / GIRL #5
BOY #1 / BOY #3 / BOY #6
BOY #2 / BOY #5
BOY #4 / BOY #7
GIRL/GIRL, BOY/BOY, OR GIRL/BOY COUPLE

(Cast this as needed for your timing and actors.)

SETTING

A room in a haunted house

TIME

October

(Setting: A room in a haunted house. There is a banquet table center stage laid out with "food" of the gross and disgusting variety. A cloche dome is also on the table with a sign next to it that reads, "Look Inside." The lights are dim, and spooky music plays.* The walls of the room have been created with black plastic, which allows for an entrance stage right, an exit stage left, and a hidden opening center stage.)

(At Rise: We hear a grinding sound and a haunted laugh from the room preceding this one, as well as surprised screams. Two people enter stage right. GIRL #1 is clinging to BOY #1 desperately.)

BOY #1. Oh my god! *(Laughing.)* You screamed so loud!

GIRL #1. Shut up! You sounded more like a girl than I did!

BOY #1. *(Examining the table.)* What do you think is in there?

GIRL #1. Don't open it! Let's just keep going!

BOY #1. What? We gotta open it!

(He reaches over and lifts the cloche. JOE's bloody head is revealed.)

See? That's not even scary. It's just –

JOE. Ahhhhhhhhh!! Help me!

(The two visitors jump back, and as they do, JENNY comes out from behind the hidden opening center stage, dressed as a demented

---

*A license to produce *Stay for Dinner* does not include a performance license for any third-party or copyrighted music. Licensees should create an original composition or use music in the public domain. For further information, please see Music Use Note on page 3.

chef. She has a bloody, plastic knife that she raises.)

JENNY. WANNA STAY FOR DINNER?!

(She chops the knife generally at the two visitors, and they scream and run to exit left. She and **JOE** *smile, then she replaces the cloche over his head and goes back to her hiding place. They wait for a moment.)*

JOE. *(Whisper-shouting.)* Pssst! Jenny!

JENNY. *(Poking her head out.)* Yeah?

JOE. Can you come here?

*(***JENNY*** comes over and lifts the cloche.)*

JENNY. Hi! *(Smiles.)*

JOE. Hi. *(Smiles.)* Can you please scratch my nose?

JENNY. *(Laughing.)* Sure! Ummm...

(She looks at her gloved hands. They have fake blood on them, and she's wary of messing up **JOE**'s *makeup. She takes the fake knife and gently scratches his nose.)*

Is that better?

JOE. Ohhhh yeah. Thank you! This stupid makeup gets so itchy.

JENNY. I know. Is it hot under there?

JOE. Yeah. It's not bad when it's busy but on slow nights I can't wait for people to open it.

(They hear a grinding sound, a haunted laugh, and screams from next door.)

JENNY. Woop! Speaking of...

(She places the cloche back on **JOE** *and runs to hide.* **GIRL #2** *and* **GIRL #3** *enter right, running and clinging to each other.)*

GIRL #2. Oh god, oh god, oh god!

GIRL #3. Chloe, why did you want to come here?!

GIRL #2. Seriously, Chloe! This sucks!

> *(They both turn to look for Chloe, assuming she is behind them.)*

GIRL #3. Chloe? Where is Chloe?

GIRL #2. Chloe! Oh god, did the clown get her?

GIRL #3. She probably ran ahead!

GIRL #2. Let's just meet at the end. I want this to be over!

GIRL #3. *(Looking at the table.)* Look inside? I don't want to.

GIRL #2. *(Shooting **GIRL #3** a dirty look.)* Fine, I'll do it. I just want to go!

> *(She opens the dome. **JOE** waits a moment and then starts to scream at them. **JENNY** comes out and stands behind them. She raises her knife.)*

JENNY. WANNA STAY FOR DINNER?!

GIRL #2 & #3. AAHHHHHH!!

> *(They run out left. As they exit, a third girl, **GIRL #4** [Chloe], comes running in stage right, screaming. She is scream-wailing the entire time she is onstage, reacting to the room around her with emphasized vocal expression. **JENNY** motions toward the exit of the room with her knife. **GIRL #4** runs to exit stage left.)*

JOE. Dang! They were just gonna leave that girl behind!

JENNY. *(Laughing.)* I know! Poor Chloe would not survive the horror movie with those two around.

JOE. Seriously. Haunted houses bring out people's true colors.

JENNY. Here, wait just a second. I have something for you.

> *(She goes back to her hiding spot, then returns with a small, battery-operated fan. She brings it back over to the table and shows **JOE**.)*

Here, I brought this after the first night. Maybe you can hold it and aim it up at your face under the table?

(She lifts the tablecloth and hands the fan to him.)

JENNY. Just push that little button.

JOE. Oh man, that's amazing! Thank you! Are you sure you don't need it?

JENNY. Nah, I'm okay. That first night they had the heat blasting but now it's fine.

JOE. Thank you so much. You're a lifesaver!

JENNY. You're welcome.

(They smile.)

JOE. So, hey, did you have fun at the party last night?

JENNY. *(Shrugging.)* Yeah, it was okay. How about you?

JOE. Yeah, it was all right.

(Pause.)

Kinda weird that we've never seen John OUT of his clown costume though, right?

JENNY. Oh my god I said the same thing! I know it was a Halloween party but why would you WANT to wear the same thing you wear here?

JOE. Maybe he really likes being a clown?

JENNY. Did you go into his guest bedroom?

JOE. No, did you?

JENNY. Yeah, he told me to put my coat in there.

(The grinding sound is heard, haunted laughter and shouts from next door.)

Hold that thought!

*(She covers **JOE** again and runs back to her hiding place. A couple enter right, fighting.)*

BOY #2. All I'm saying is that you could have TOLD me Evan was going with you to the movie.

GIRL #5. It was a big group! I didn't think it mattered. There were other guys there too.

BOY #2. Yeah, but you haven't DATED those other guys.

GIRL #5. Can we just please enjoy the haunted house? You've been begging me to go!

BOY #2. Okay fine, here we go.

(*Looking at the table.*) Oh, they want me to open this dome? Gee, I wonder what could be underneath?

(*Lifts cloche.*)

Oh, a bloody head? Imagine that!

JOE. AHHHHHH!! HELP ME!!

(**GIRL #5** *jumps.*)

BOY #2. Oooooohhh it's screaming at me. Big freakin' whoop.

(**JENNY** *comes out from her hiding place.*)

JENNY. WANNA STAY FOR DINNER?!

(**GIRL #5** *jumps toward* **BOY #2**.)

BOY #2. Oh, surprise, surprise! This place sucks!

GIRL #5. Can't you have fun? You're making tonight horrible!

(**GIRL #5** *and* **BOY #2** *begin to exit left.*)

BOY #2. Oh, I'm sorry. Maybe you'd be having more fun if EVAN were here!

(**GIRL #5** *and* **BOY #2** *exit.*)

JENNY. Something tells me they're not gonna make it.

JOE. Yeah, I wouldn't want to be in their car on the ride home.

(*Pause.*)

So, anyway, what was in John the clown's bedroom?

JENNY. Oh, right! It was totally covered in clown stuff. Like, posters, dolls, all kinds of crazy stuff. It was so creepy.

JOE. Oh god! Like guests have to sleep with a bunch of clowns staring at them?

JENNY. Yeah. Can you imagine?

JOE. You couldn't pay me to sleep in a room like that.

JENNY. Also, I wonder if he EVER wears normal clothes? What if he goes to his day job dressed as a clown?

JOE. *(Laughing.)* Like he's a lawyer and he shows up in court with a red nose and size-twenty shoes?

JENNY. *(Laughing.)* Exactly!

> *(Pause.)*

Oh man, I wonder what he DOES do for a living.

JOE. Maybe we should have known more about him before going to his house...

JENNY. Yeah maybe...

JOE. I was kinda bummed you and I didn't get to hang out more last night.

JENNY. Yeah... I looked for you, but you seemed like you were in a deep conversation so...

JOE. Deep conversation? With who?

JENNY. Lisa. *(Mocking.)* The sexy vampire.

JOE. Oh. Yeah, we talked for a little bit. She was asking for advice because she got into a fight with her boyfriend.

JENNY. Oh, she has a boyfriend?

JOE. Yeah.

> *(Pause.)*

Your boyfriend looked like a nice guy, by the way.

JENNY. *My* boyfriend?

JOE. Yeah, I wouldn't have chosen the whole Superman costume, you know, it's so cliché but he seemed nice.

JENNY. *(Laughing.)* Ummm, that was my *brother.*

JOE. Your brother?

JENNY. Yeah.

JOE. So, what you're saying, is that we both avoided each other the whole evening even though we actually wanted to hang out?

JENNY. I think that's what we're both saying.

JOE. That seems dumb.

JENNY. Yeah, it does.

> *(The grinding sound is heard, haunted laughter and shouts from next door. They*

both want to say something, but they need to get ready, so **JENNY** *covers* **JOE**'s *head and runs to her hiding place.* **BOY #3** *and* **BOY #4** *enter right, grasping at each other, completely terrified. They see the sign and neither one of them wants to open it. After a series of non-verbal sounds, muttering, and gestures,* **BOY #3** *pushes* **BOY #4** *to open it.* **BOY #4** *starts to shakily move toward the cloche, trying to gather his courage to lift it, but* **BOY #3** *scares him by pushing him toward the cloche, and they both scream and run out. After a moment,* **JENNY** *cautiously peeks out and sees that they are gone. She lifts the cloche.)*

JOE. Ahhhhhhhh– Oh! It's you. What happened?

JENNY. They decided not to open it.

JOE. We really need to figure out a plan B when they decide not to do that...

JENNY. Yeah, I'm never sure if I should still come out or what...

JOE. We should probably ask Reggie about that.

JENNY. Probably.

(Pause.)

So...anyway...

JOE. So, the party... What if we have a do-over? Let's pretend we're at the party again. There's creepy clown shit everywhere and John the serial killer just gave us some punch. Hi.

JENNY. Hi.

JOE. You look pretty.

JENNY. I was dressed as a zombie cheerleader.

JOE. Still.

JENNY. *(Smiling.)* Thanks. You don't look so bad yourself.

JOE. Why yes, I do look handsome, don't I?

JENNY. And so modest!

JOE. Of course!

> *(They laugh and pause, smiling at each
> other.)*

You know, if we HAD hung out last night, I wonder
what would have happened.

JENNY. What do you mean?

JOE. Like, I *feel* like if we *had* started talking, we might not
have stopped.

JENNY. Oh yeah?

JOE. Yeah. And maybe we would have had such a good time
talking that I would have offered you a ride home.

JENNY. Then what?

JOE. Well, maybe we wouldn't have wanted to go home yet,
so maybe we would have gone to the diner and had
midnight pancakes.

JENNY. I love midnight pancakes.

JOE. Me too. Then, maybe I would have driven you home,
but we wouldn't have wanted the night to end yet.

JENNY. Maybe I would have invited you in to watch a
movie.

JOE. Yeah? And maybe, it would be a scary movie and you'd
get scared and I'd have to protect you.

JENNY. Or maybe YOU'D get scared and I'D have to protect
YOU.

JOE. *(Smiling.)* Either way.

JENNY. *(Leaning in.)* So, now that we're so close, you know,
protecting each other, what happens next?

JOE. Well, then –

> *(They're interrupted by the grinding sound,
> the haunted laugh, and shouts from the room
> next door.)*

JENNY. Dammit!

> *(They both look pained as **JENNY** puts the
> cloche back and runs to her hiding place. **BOY**
> **#5**, **BOY #6**, and **BOY #7** enter right, pushing*

each other and making fun of how they're reacting to the haunted house. They see the table.)

BOY #5. Dude, YOU open it, bro!

*(He pushes **BOY #6** toward the table.)*

BOY #6. I don't want to open it, bro!

BOY #7. Chicken, bro?!

*(He makes chicken sounds, mocking **BOY #6**.)*

BOY #6. Whatever, bro!

(He confidently saunters over to the table and lifts the cloche.)

It's just a fake head. This place is so lame, bro!

BOY #7. *(Crossing over to **JOE**.)* Dare me to touch it, bro?

BOY #5. Yeah, bro!

*(**BOY #7** creeps over to the table to touch **JOE**, but as he reaches out, **JOE** starts screaming. The guys laugh, and **BOY #5** holds up a cell phone for a selfie as they all gather around **JOE**, making faces at the camera. **JENNY** comes out of her hiding place.)*

JENNY. WANNA STAY FOR DINNER?!

*(The guys startle at her entrance, and **BOY #6** slams the cloche back down on **JOE**'s head. **JENNY** chases them offstage, knife raised as they scream and exit. **JENNY** rushes over to **JOE**.)*

Are you okay? Stupid jerks.

JOE. Yeah, I'm fine. I think they messed up my makeup though.

JENNY. Let me see.

(She leans in and takes off her glove to smooth part of his makeup on his face.)

Good as new.

(She takes this opportunity to stay close to him.)

JENNY. So, about last night... What would have happened next?

JOE. Well, if we were watching a scary movie, and we were super close, kind of like this...

JENNY. Yes?

JOE. I might have kissed you.

JENNY. Yeah?

JOE. Yeah. Actually...if I wasn't stuck in a table, I would kiss you right now.

JENNY. Really?

JOE. Really.

JENNY. Well, since you *are* stuck in a table, I suppose *I* will just have to kiss *you*.

JOE. Okay.

JENNY. Okay.

*(They both smile as **JENNY** leans in and they kiss. She pulls back, they both grin, and she leans in to kiss him some more. A grinding sound is heard, haunted laughter, and screams from next door. They continue to kiss as another couple, **BOY/GIRL**, **GIRL/GIRL**, or **BOY/BOY** enter right. The couple runs in, looking behind them, then checks out the weird scene in front of them. They look at each other, confused. Then they sneak off stage left, possibly throwing out a "Woo Hoo!" or something similar as they exit and the lights fade.)*

(Curtain.)

Bunkmates

Jeff Ronan

BUNKMATES premiered as part of the 44th Annual Samuel French Off Off Broadway Short Play Festival at the Vineyard Theatre in New York City on August 20, 2019. The director and sound designer was Ben Liebert, with sound engineering by Luke Weyand. The cast was as follows:

SHELLEY...Alesandra Nahodil

GARY .... Paul Peglar

CHARACTERS

SHELLEY – thirties, thick South Carolina accent, bright and full of life
GARY – thirties, thick Jersey accent, nerdy but unaware of it

SETTING

Shelley and Gary's homes and survival bunkers

TIME

The months leading up to and following January 1, 2000

(The sound of a dial-up modem.)

(Lights reveal **SHELLEY** *seated at her home computer. She's dressed in nineties fashion. Thick South Carolina accent.)*

(Note: Computers can be physically realized, mimed, or simply alluded to through the dialogue.)

SHELLEY. Subject: Y2 *Not* OK. Exclamation point, exclamation point, exclamation point...

(She considers.)

...exclamation point: Hello there fellow believers. This is in response to CamperDad22's post that he was preparing for Y2K with a weekend's worth of supplies. That is – repeat – a *single* weekend for himself, his wife, and his children. Well, CamperDad22, I hope you've *also* prepared for when Monday rolls around and they ask why you didn't love them enough to keep them alive. Anything less than a year's worth of proper utilities is a slap in the face to your loved ones. I have stocked my shelter with ten FDA-approved fifty-five-gallon drums of water, a two-years' supply of canned food, and kibble and insulin for my dog, Ruffles, who has canine diabetes, bless his heart. I hope everyone is taking this upcoming, catastrophic event more seriously.

(The sound of a dial-up modem. Lights reveal **GARY** *seated at his home computer. Nineties fashion. Un-hip glasses. Thick Jersey accent.)*

GARY. Reply to TheseBootsWereMadeForDancing17's message Y2 *Not* OK exclamation point, exclamation point, exclamation point, exclamation point: I totally agree. Anyone not taking *at least* those measures is not

going to live to see 2001. And no, I am not referring to
the Stanley Kubrick seminal film classic, JK. Haha. But
I am *not* K about taking proper precautionary measures.
I have a survival bunker of my own, provisions for three
years, and have recently completed a wildlife survival
boot camp. Stay safe out there, believers!

SHELLEY. Reply to You'reMyOnlyHope77: What kind of
wildlife survival boot camp did you take? I hadn't
thought of doing one but am intrigued. Do tell more.

GARY. Private message to TheseBootsWereMadeFor
Dancing17: I hope you don't mind me taking my
response off of the public forum, but I would rather
not have this information out there for the naysayers to
see. My wildlife survival boot camp was self-taught. In
the woods behind my backyard I managed to live off of
the land for ten straight hours where I foraged for food
and built a temporary shelter out of a fallen fir tree. I
would have stayed out longer but it was pretty cold and
it started to get dark. If Y2K is as bad as I fear, I want
to make sure once it's safe to come out that I have the
necessary skills to survive in the aftermath.

SHELLEY. Private message to You'reMyOnlyHope77:
Practicing survival skills is smart thinking. I did not
consider what state the world might be left in once we
can leave our shelters. And self-taught, at that! You
sound very rugged.

GARY. *(Adjusting his glasses.)* I guess you could say that.

SHELLEY. Are you rural? I'm in South Carolina, myself.

GARY. New Jersey. Though we have more forests than people
expect. I'm Gary, by the way.

SHELLEY. I'm Shelley.

GARY. It's very nice to meet you, Shelley.

SHELLEY. E-mail to BeamMeUp66: Dear Gary, Shelley here.
Thank you for sharing your e-mail address with me.
Two months away until the big 2000! I thought you'd
be pleased to know I completed my own backyard boot
camp last night, though I did get some stares from

my next-door neighbor Linda. I got scared around midnight when I heard growls in the bushes, but it was just Linda's good-for-nothing teenage son Lonnie pretending to be a black bear.

LONNIE. *(Offstage.)* Oh no, Shelley, the bear's back! Rawr rawr rawr!

> (**SHELLEY** *rises and shuts the window, shutting out* **LONNIE**'s *voice.*)

SHELLEY. He teased me for a while, but I knew that you would think it was the right thing to do, and that helped me make it through the night, thinking of you. It's nice having a friend who doesn't tease me. Sincerely, Shelley from South Carolina.

GARY. E-mail to SassyShel17: Dear Shelley, thank you for reaching out. I think it is very admirable to beef up your survival skills for the upcoming outage, especially in the face of mockery from naysayers like Lonnie. He sounds like a real A-hole, pardon my language. I for one am proud of you, and am glad to hear I had some small part in helping. All the best, Gary from Jersey. P.S. How is Ruffles' canine diabetes? And what kind of dog are they?

SHELLEY. Hi Gary, thank you for asking after Ruffles. He is a nineteen-year-old Labradoodle, as spry as the day I got him. Outside of his canine diabetes he is the picture of health. The vet says he is a medical abnormality and could either die tomorrow or live another ten years. I consider him my good luck charm and he keeps me fit trying to keep up with him on our walks. Do you have any pets? Your friend, Shelley.

GARY. Hi Shelley, I have two Scottish Fold cats, Mulder and Scully. I inherited them when they were kittens from my Aunt Debbie, who moved to Canada with her girlfriend four and a half years ago. Mulder likes to eat my mail and Scully is terrified of vegetables, especially zucchini. They are a couple of nuts and I love them. Do you have any plans on how to keep Ruffles exercised during your stay in your bunker? Mulder and Scully don't need a lot of room thankfully, but I'm experimenting with building a large hamster wheel-type contraption for them to run in. They do not enjoy the Cat Wheel so far, but I'm still tinkering with the design, and the name. Your friend, Gary.

SHELLEY. Hi Gary, what about the Catawampus? Or the Caterwauler? Either way, I love the idea so I moved my stationary bike out to the bunker and rigged up a tiny treadmill to connect to it, so that as I pedal, the treadmill will go, allowing Ruffles to run on it as I ride. You should have seen how happy he looked on it! Your friend, Shelley.

GARY. Hi Shelley, I love the word Catawampus, though I had to look up what it meant. And your contraption sounds ingenious! I sure would love to see it in motion sometime. Your friend, Gary.

    (Long beat.)

Hi Shelley, hope all is well with you and Ruffles as you head into December! Gary.

    (Long beat.)

Hey, Shelley, hope you are okay. Reading back through my previous e-mails I wanted to clarify that I simply meant the device you built sounded really neat and I would love to see how it worked, maybe in a video. I hope it didn't sound like I was trying to invite myself over. Haha. Your friend, Gary.

    (Quick beat.)

Hey Shelley, just to clarify once more. I also hope it didn't sound like I was saying I would love to see you riding the stationary bike in, like, a sexual manner. That is not at all what I meant. I have a deep respect for you and would hate if I have somehow insulted you. Your *platonic* friend, Gary.

SHELLEY. Gary! Hi! Sorry for the delayed response. Ruffles chewed through a wire and triggered the lockdown on my bunker while I was stocking the shelves. Been stuck there all weekend until the mailman came by and heard me hollering. All is okay now. Also, you have nothing to worry about. I understand what you meant by your previous e-mail. But just so you know, I would not mind you seeing me ride my stationary bike. You could watch me ride my stationary bike any time.

> *(Embarrassed beat.)*

Hahaha, okay, anyway, looking forward to continuing our correspondence. Your friend...backspace, backspace...

> *(Thinking.)*

Your...*currently* platonic friend, Shelley.

> *(Beat.)*

Smiley face.

GARY. Hi, Shelley – Your good friend, Gary.

SHELLEY. Hi Gary – Your good friend, Shelley.

GARY. Shelley – Gary.

SHELLEY. Gary – Shelley.

GARY. Shel– Gar.

SHELLEY. Gar– Shel.

> *(Beat.)*

GARY. Shelley...*yours*, Gary.

SHELLEY. *(Touched.)* Gary... *Always* yours, Shelley.

> *(They both grin.)*

GARY. Hi Shel, wanted to give you a heads-up that I'm powering down my computer leading up to New Year's. My buddy J.T. said that when Y2K comes, any electronics still plugged in have the risk of shooting electricity through a man's testicles and pulverizing his sperm count. I figure better safe than sorry. Will that be okay? Yours, Gary.

SHELLEY. Hi Gar, I understand, though I'm sorry to hear I'll no longer have a way to chat with you. I must admit I have gotten used to our daily correspondence and will be sorry to, as they say, "sign off." Yours, Shelley.

GARY. Shelley, I hope you did not take my previous e-mail as a goodbye. I just meant that we would need to find another way to communicate. Do you happen to know Morse code and/or own a telegraph key and ham radio? If so I have a telegraph key of my own that I purchased off of eBay and would love to continue our correspondence. Yours, Gary.

SHELLEY. Gary, I have an old ham radio, but unfortunately don't know Morse code or own a telegraph key. Wish I did! Yours, Shelley.

GARY. Shelley, no problem! I've just mailed you a telegraph key and Morse code booklet. It is very easy to learn. Consider it an early Christmas gift. Yours, Gary.

> *(They now communicate with Morse code by tapping on a telegraph key which is or isn't mimed. It takes a while for* **SHELLEY** *to get the hang of it.)*

SHELLEY. *(Slow, halting.)* Gary...guess who? It is...Shelley. Still...getting...the hang of...Morste...Cote.

GARY. Shelley, you are doing great for your first time. Very happy to be able to continue our correspondence. One week and counting.

SHELLEY. Any...special plans...for New Year's Eve?

GARY. Just me, Mulder, and Scully. Yourself?

SHELLEY. Just me...and Ruffles. Wish...you could be here... in person.

GARY. Me too. I would invite you here, but I didn't think to prep the bunker for two.

SHELLEY. Same here.

GARY. Maybe once it is safe to come out again we could meet?

SHELLEY. I would like that...very much.

> *(A shift. Light music plays.* * **SHELLEY** *has gotten better at Morse code.)*

A license to produce Bunkmates *does not include a performance license for any third-party or copyrighted music. Licensees should create an original composition or use music in the public domain. For further information, please see Music Use Note on page 3.

GARY. Happy New Year's Eve, Shelley! Hope you're all set for the lockdown. We're powered down and me and the cats are ready for the new year! Yourself?

SHELLEY. Happy New Year's Eve to you, Gary! Ruffles and I are also settled in here. He's wrapped up in his favorite blanket and I have a Nancy Sinatra record playing on my battery-operated record player.

GARY. That sounds magical. I'm currently lifting a glass of champagne to you, Shelley.

SHELLEY. And I to you, Gary.

GARY. Five minutes to midnight!

SHELLEY. Three minutes to midnight!

GARY. One minute to midnight!

SHELLEY. Whatever happens Gary, I'm glad I found you.

GARY. Me too, Shelley.

SHELLEY. Happy New Year, Gary!

GARY. Happy New Year, Shelley!

> *(The friendly woof of a nineteen-year-old Labradoodle.)*

SHELLEY. Ruffles says Happy New Year too!

GARY. Happy New Year, Ruffles!

> *(Anxious beat.)*

SHELLEY. What do you think it's like outside?

GARY. I guess...we'll just have to wait and see.

> *(Another shift. A montage.)*

SHELLEY. Got any threes?

GARY. I've got one three. Got any eights?

SHELLEY. Go fish.

GARY. I rolled a four.

SHELLEY. That's Park Avenue, you owe me rent!

GARY. Okay...I think it's Professor Plum...in the conservatory... with the revolver.

SHELLEY. Nope!

GARY. D7.

SHELLEY. Miss.

GARY. D8.

SHELLEY. Hit!

GARY. C8.

SHELLEY. Gary, you sank my battleship! Good game.

GARY. Good game.

SHELLEY. Gary, I have been thinking. It has been a few months now and my neighbor Linda has been by a few times to knock on my bunker, even though I told her she should stay indoors. She was saying that everything is normal on the outside. That besides a few technical mishaps everyone has been fine. I think it might be safe to go out.

GARY. I would seriously advise against that Shelley. Who knows how many nuclear reactors and government facilities were affected by Y2K? We don't know what kind of radiation or contagions might have been unleashed. Did you actually see Linda?

SHELLEY. No, she just yelled through the door, but she's got a big, loud voice so I heard her fine.

GARY. For all we know, the radiation could have affected her brain and she only *thinks* everything is normal. How many more months of supplies do you have?

SHELLEY. A little over a year and a half.

GARY. Then that's how long you should wait.

SHELLEY. Well, what if we boot our computers back up to do some research?

GARY. I told you about the electric currents. I cannot risk my sperm count, Shelley! And for all we know, the effect of the electricity on your ovaries could be devastating!

SHELLEY. I can worry about my own ovaries, thank you very much!

GARY. Sorry.

SHELLEY. Gary, what if it's actually safe to leave our bunkers? Don't you want to see me in person some day?

GARY. Of course, but we can't risk it. It's safer to wait.

SHELLEY. Well how much longer do you think you'll wait?

GARY. Until it's safe.

SHELLEY. And how will you know that?

GARY. When I know, I'll know.

SHELLEY. Well I hope you do know, Gary. 'Cause I'm not stayin' in this bunker forever.

(Lights go out on **SHELLEY** *and she disappears.)*

GARY. Shelley, was wondering if you were around. I owe you a rematch in Battleship.

(Beat.)

And you owe me a rematch in Go Fish. Haha.

(Beat.)

Are you there, Shelley? How is Ruffles?

(Beat.)

Shelley, if you're there, can you please respond so I know you're okay?

(He thinks for a moment. The sound of a dial-up modem is heard again. He shields his crotch with one hand and types with the other.)

E-mail to SassyShel17: Dear Shelley, I've had a lot of time to think the past few days and I wanted to say you were right. I do want to meet you in person and continue to get to know the incredible woman you are. But I don't know if I'm brave enough right now. It's only a single door that separates me and you, though admittedly, one that is bulletproof and has fourteen separate locks. One day I'll be able to open that door. Until then, I hope you can be patient with me. Forever yours, Gary.

(Thinking.) Backspace, backspace.

(Long beat.)

Love...Gary

(The whoosh of an e-mail being sent. **GARY** *stares out, waiting for a response. A long moment passes. Suddenly, a door buzzer rings. He looks up, confused.)*

GARY. Hello...?

(Another buzz. **GARY**, *scared but hopeful, rises and cautiously steps forward.)*

Shelley?

(No response. **GARY** *nervously undoes an elaborate lock. And another. And twelve more. He takes a deep breath and opens the heavy door. The warm light of the outdoors spills onto his face, and a nineteen-year-old Labradoodle lets out a friendly woof.* **GARY** *smiles.)*

Cluck Deluxe

Bonnie Antosh

CLUCK DELUXE premiered as part of the 44th Annual Samuel French Off Off Broadway Short Play Festival at the Vineyard Theatre in New York City on August 20, 2019. The director was Molly Clifford. The cast was as follows:

ISA . . . . Anissa Comonte

STEPH . . . . Mariette Strauss

LILI . . . . Avery Deutsch

CHARACTERS

ISA – Grew up in Mississippi, charismatic, loyal, drinks Pepsi. 24-29.

STEPH – Raised in the Hudson Valley, holds herself to high standards, drinks ginger ale (maybe, only on special occasions). 24-29.

LILI – Designed to sound trustworthy and sell you things.

SETTING

A car
traveling down a highway
Mississippi

TIME

A few days before Thanksgiving

AUTHOR'S NOTES

A midline double slash (//) indicates overlapping dialogue.
A line-ending double slash (//) indicates no pause between speakers.
A dash (–) indicates a suspension or the decision not to finish a thought.

For beats of silence:
Hot versus cool indicates tension or ease.
Minute versus second indicates duration.

(Suggestions of the front seat of a car. Snack graveyard. Empty Big Gulp cup and water bottle in the cup holders. Balled-up hoodie under the passenger seat.)

*(**ISA** drives, and **STEPH** rides with her feet up on the dash. Jams on the stereo.* **LILI** sleeps in the back seat.)*

(They ride in silence for a few seconds.)

STEPH. I kill your // cows!

ISA. I kill your // no!

STEPH. Into the grave, Bessie!

ISA. SmashaBABY, how'd you get so good at roadtrip games //

STEPH. *(Cracking up.)* Smash – what'd you just say?

ISA. Ughh, I'm practicing not cursing.

STEPH. Seriously?

ISA. So serious. I normal cussed last Thanksgiving,
    just like "o shit" when – sh– stuff fell on the floor,
    and my grandma got really upset and it made her cry.

STEPH. Grams!

ISA. Yeah, crying grandmas. No joke. I stress-ate a *lot* of pie.

STEPH. She's really that Baptist?

ISA. She's that Baptist.
    She won't even do the champagne toasts at weddings.

STEPH. And – she knows I'm coming for Thanksgiving?

ISA. Of course.

STEPH. I don't wanna kill your grammy with a heart attack...

---

*A license to produce *Cluck Deluxe* does not include a performance license for any third-party or copyrighted music. Licensees should create an original composition or use music in the public domain. For further information, please see Music Use Note on page 3.

ISA. She's gonna be civil.
She'll be like "bless your heart" civil.

–

Don't worry. She's a very loving person.

     (A hot second.)

STEPH. And she doesn't think I'm like your orphan roommate?

ISA. No, she knows we *moved-in*. Together.

STEPH. *(Not totally convinced.)* Okay.

–

Oh! My mom texted this morning and she said, quote:
All-caps hi Stephie bon voyage travel safe don't forget to buy thank-you flowers for Isa's parents four exclamation marks!!!!
She was probably day drunk.
And also she demands that you stay at least half a week at Christmas.

ISA. Well, please tell your mom that I am quote:
Amenable to extended stay in Hudson Valley as long as she makes The Eleven Cheese //

STEPH. Twelve Cheese //

ISA. Twelve Cheese Scallion Dip. And four exclamation marks!!!!

     (A cool second.)

STEPH. Ooof, I can*not* stop eating these clementines! You want one?

ISA. Nah, let's stop for actual lunch. My foot's cramping up.

STEPH. How much further?

ISA. Like two hours, three hours if there's traffic? What's the map –

STEPH. *(Talking into the phone, over-enunciating.)* LiLi, how many miles to Jackson?

LILI. *(Waking up.)* Sorry, I didn't get that.

STEPH. How. Many. Miles. From. Here. To. Jackson. Mississippi?

LILI. Let's take a detour to Belzoni, Mississippi: Home of the World's Biggest Shrimp!!
Visit the Old Spanish // Fort.

STEPH. LiLi, turn on maps!

LILI. Mississippi: Birthplace of Pine-Sol and Kermit the Frog!

STEPH. Maps!

LILI. Mississippi! Recalculating! Mississippi! Where you can drink a beer while operating a motor vehicle //

STEPH. Shut up!

LILI. *(Undaunted.)* Pull over and grab an ice-cold //

STEPH. TURN OFF!
Damn, why's your phone so messed up?

ISA. I sortof – ugggh – half-knocked it into the toilet last week. Since then, LiLi has just gotten really shameless about ads.

STEPH. *(Talking into the phone, over-enunciating.)* Stop. Being. Shameless. About. Ads.
–
Is that true? Can you drink *literally* while you drive in Mississippi?

ISA. Yeah, home sweet home.

STEPH. How is that real?

ISA. Honestly, I would fluffin' love a beer and a biscuit right now.

STEPH. Doesn't that seem criminally negligent?

ISA. Nah! Come on, you love it!
Everyone kicking back in five-o'clock traffic //

STEPH. Is that like – leftover from when people drove horse and buggies? 'Cause that's probably not even safe, drunk driving a buggy.

ISA. I mean, you're not allowed to drive *drunk* //

STEPH. Right, just *buzzed*. So you can blithely slaughter people on the highway, then –
That's an indefensibly crazy law.

(A hot minute.)

ISA. So what about lunch?

STEPH. Well I think we should really commit in either direction like,

salad or Cinnabon.

ISA. What's at this exit?

STEPH. *(Reading highway sign.)* There's a sign coming up. Okay, we got:

FakeBurgerMonarchy

FakeBurgerScaryClown

FakeItalianBreadstickFeast

FakeMexicanCrunchadilla

FakeChineseTinyPanda

Cinnabon!!

–

And Cluck Deluxe.

ISA. *(Blast from the past.)* Cluck Deluxe? That was my after-school *spot*!

I haven't been there since I was like seventeen.

STEPH. Good.

ISA. That's *obviously* the choice. Cluck Deluxe! Their curly fries are God.

STEPH. You're kidding, yeah?

ISA. Well not – God. But stupid delicious. LiLi, add stop at Cluck Deluxe!

LILI. Adding stop // at Cluck –

STEPH. LiLi, turn off!

I would rather eat a breaded

fried

rat

than give a single cent of my money to those – *chicken fiends.*

ISA. Did you get food poisoned there?

LILI. Exit for Cluck Deluxe in 200 feet!

STEPH. *(Laughably obvious.)* No, Isa, that restaurant is run by hateful bigots!

ISA. Ummm, one of my BFFs used to be a manager at Cluck's and she gave everyone free milkshakes //

STEPH. Well I hope one-of-your-BFFs doesn't hate Queer America like the CEO of her workplace obviously does.

ISA. Wasn't that whole controversy like ten years ago?

STEPH. It was four years ago – and those same ignorant people are still growing rich off blood chicken.

ISA. You don't have to agree with someone's politics to eat at their fast-casual restaurant.

STEPH. Absolutely not, but //

LILI. Absolutely not too late to turn off for // Cluck –

STEPH. LiLi, stop being an agent of Corporate Satan!

(**LILI** *flips* **STEPH** *off.*)

Okay, that's true, but why would I go out of my way to support that kind of business? A fast-food monstrosity run by people who have loudly and proudly proclaimed their hatred for *both of us*?

ISA. I mean, they're entitled to their beliefs //

STEPH. But they're not entitled to my money.

ISA. Fair. Okay.

–

Let's just – stop somewhere quick. You can grab your Cinnabon-slash-salad. And then we'll go through the drive-thru at Cluck Deluxe so I can get my curly fries.

(A very hot minute.)

STEPH. Are you trolling // me?

ISA. You don't have to eat a single fry!

STEPH. Were you not paying attention to anything I just said?

ISA. I get it. I respect your choice not to eat at Cluck Deluxe, and you need to respect my decision to want some curly fries after driving seven hours.

(A hot second.)

STEPH. Do you watch Woody Allen movies?

ISA. What?

STEPH. Do you watch movies directed by Woody Allen?

ISA. No, I have never seen a Woody Allen movie in all – actually, that's a lie. I did try to watch one of the old ones flying back from Carmen's wedding, but the first ten minutes were too boring. Even for a plane.

STEPH. But do you believe that we should hold people accountable for their words and deeds?

ISA. Okay, that's an enormous question, and honestly, I'm talking about drive-thru chicken.

STEPH. Right, but you don't want to see how your small, independent choices have power, right? When people unambiguously say that they *hate* you, why won't you believe them?

ISA. I don't think the CEO of Cluck Deluxe has ever even said that he *hates* lesbians!

STEPH. Right, he just donates money to curtail our legal rights and fight against the notion that we're equally human and worthy of love.

ISA. I mean, that obviously sucks, but I just don't see that reflected in the actual restaurants. Like the people who work at Cluck Deluxe are literally the friendliest people in all of fast food.

STEPH. Would they be that nice if we walked in holding hands?

ISA. I dunno! Probably most of them would and a few wouldn't. That's just standard Mississippi, though.

STEPH. And you just accept that? You know better, and you have a duty to call out that backwards, reactionary // shit.

ISA. Can you please have spent more than two seconds below the Mason-Dixon Line before deciding that an entire *state* is backwards?

STEPH. Umm you complain about your hometown all the // time.

ISA. Have I *ever* come out swinging at you over some subtle-racist soccer mom who's wine drunk on the Metro-North? No, I would never // put that on you.

STEPH. But all you have to do is give up a chicken sandwich and some fries!

ISA. How come I have to sacrifice every part of me that you don't like?

STEPH. Because fries and highway beer aren't real sacrifices! The personal is political!

ISA. You think I don't fucking know that? That's why I'm taking my girlfriend home, even though it's gonna freak my family the fuck out and make my grandma break down in the // bathroom!

STEPH. RED LIGHT!

> *(A loud truck horn. The car screeches to a halt, throwing* **STEPH** *and* **ISA** *forward in their seats.)*
>
> *(A hot second.)*

You okay?

ISA. I'm okay.

–

Are you okay?

STEPH. I'm fine. Just – pull over. There's a gas station right here.

> *(They pull over and park. They're really shaken up.)*

I'm sorry I almost made you crash by arguing about chicken.

ISA. It wasn't your fault.

STEPH. You should go to Cluck Deluxe. If you want.

ISA. No, it's okay. I feel kindof sick from –
Maybe their curly fries are only good 'cause – devil magic.

STEPH. One part corn oil, one part virgin blood sacrifice.

–

I just

I want us to be on the same team.

ISA. I know.

We are – most of the time.

STEPH. I can fly home.

ISA. No //

STEPH. Not in a martyr-y way. I don't want to mess with your family's // time together.

ISA. Hey, hey, hey. You're my family too. They're getting that. They want you here.

(A hot second.)

Just – one thing, though.

STEPH. I know, I won't talk about the primaries.

ISA. That's actually not what I was // gonna –

STEPH. The problematic nature of Thanksgiving?

ISA. Heard, but //

STEPH. My ignorance of football?

ISA. Yeah, my mom will for *sure* judge you for that. But – you just – you can't tell them how much you hate Cluck Deluxe. Okay? My siblings will run you out of the house and tell the neighbors that you're horribly disfigured.

STEPH. Okay, I promise. But we're gonna keep talking about this on the ride home.

ISA. If it's actually –

If it's not just –

STEPH. It's not.

–

And I promise not to drink around your grammy.

ISA. That's a terrible promise. Even I can't deal with my grandma sober.

STEPH. Okay. Noted.

(They start to pull out of the gas station.)

ISA. *(Talking into phone.)* LiLi, fastest route to Jackson.

LILI. You are on the fastest route to Jackson, Mississippi!
Jackson, Rhode Island!
Jackson, Wyoming!

You will arrive in approximately twenty-six hours and //

STEPH. Wait. Do you wanna –

ISA. What?

STEPH. Take a detour to see
The World's Biggest Shrimp?

*(A warm second. **LILI** celebrates her triumph.)*

ISA. I mean – when in Mississippi, baby!

(Tires screech as lights fade.)

I Love You
St. Petersburg!

Bixby Elliot

I LOVE YOU ST. PETERSBURG! premiered as part of the 44th Annual Samuel French Off Off Broadway Short Play Festival at the Vineyard Theatre in New York City on August 20, 2019, produced by Theater Husband/Theater Wife Project. The director was Jack Dentinger, and the costume designer was Oliva Vaughn Hern. The cast was as follows:

SALLY . . . . Erin Layton

I LOVE YOU ST. PETERSBURG! was originally developed at the Cherry Picking Festival at the Wild Project in New York City. The reading was directed by Clare Mottola and performed by Nicole Golden.

CHARACTERS

SALLY – Female-presenting, late thirties/early forties mother of two. Any race.

SETTING

A blank stage

TIME

Late afternoon

*(**SALLY** stands center stage.)*
(She holds a stack of index cards.)
(She looks out at the crowd.)
(She is nervous – to say the least.)
(Silence.)
(Silence.)
(Silence.)

SALLY. This is fun.

(It isn't.)

Wow. Huh? Super fun!

Right?

I feel like a celebrity.

Like – I don't know – like Madonna.

Wait. Do you know her?

Blond Ambition.

No?

I need my sunglasses – the lights are so blinding.

(Laughs at herself. No one else does. Trying to relax. Failing.)

(Looking down at an index card...)

Okay. Right.

I wrote some things down.

A few "prompts." Ha. Okay.

(Reading.) "Say something about yourself."

Yes. Yes!

Okay.

I, um, I – purple is my favorite color.

Let's give it up for purple!

(No reaction from crowd.)

I am crazy for broccoli – I could eat it all day.

Steamed – with some – I don't know – olive oil!

(Looking at crowd.)

Okay. No broccoli lovers – should have guessed that.

(Beat.)

Airplanes make me horny.

Okay. No. That – that is not appropriate.

(Beat.)

Let's strike that last part. Forget I said that.

Not that I want to make you ashamed of your sexuality – that is not – you should feel free to explore whatever sexual urges you may have – on an airplane or a bus or a...

(She looks over at an unseen person.)

Or nowhere – nowhere. Sex is bad.

(Beat. Looks at card.)

Okay. Right. I should have said.

(Formally.) Thank you Ms. Cohen for inviting me here to Ridge Valley Elementary's: First Grade Career Day.

(Beat.)

I am really honored and excited *(A lie.)* to be here.

I am *(Pointing to a child.)* I am the mother of – of – well.

Sorry. I know it. I do.

Johnafer. HA. No.

Jonathan.

My daughter's name is Jennifer.

She's eight. I remember that. I know that.

Although – Johanfer – that's good. Like Bennifer for Ben Affleck and Jennifer Lopez – or – well Jennifer Garner – well – either – or – rather, neither anymore – he can't keep a Jennifer to save his life, right?

(Laughing, then...)

(Looking over at Ms. Cohen.)

Yes. Career Day! Awesome. I am happy to be here for career day.

(Beat.)

Although. I must say.

It does seem a bit early to be – well – to be so focused on careers.

You should be playing...

(Sing-songy.) Red Rover. Red Rover. Send – what's your name?

(No answer.)

Send quiet girl with the braces right over. HA.

(Beat.)

I had braces. They hurt like hell.

No. No. They did not.

Okay. Your teeth are going to look gorgeous!

Dental Care! Hooray!

(Quick beat.)

Career Day.

So. Sure. Career Day.

When Ms. Cohen called me up – I was like – me? You want me to come to career day? I said, "Did that mom whose son gave everyone lice last year cancel at the last minute" and she was like..."Yes. Dr. Janice Stern is performing emergency brain surgery tomorrow"...and I was like –

"Next best thing. ME!"

(Quick beat.)

I am NOT a brain surgeon. Although I did contemplate that at one point.

But that takes about 200 years of school and who wants that – I mean school sucks.

(Quick beat.)

But – I love school. School is great.

Stay in school!

I also wanted to be a veterinarian.

A photo stylist.

A garbage man – woman. Moved on from that.

An activist.

I would have made such a great activist. Like Sally Field in *Norma Rae*!

(Marching.) I AM MAD AS HELL AND I AM NOT GOING TO TAKE IT ANYMORE.

EVERYONE! I AM... *(Beat.)* wait. Wrong movie.

I ended up going to school and majoring in communications, that's sort of what you do when you don't know what you want to do but you have to declare something. I thought.

I can communicate – I'll be a communications major.

And then I spent most of my time dating Izzy Geller and getting drunk with Elizabeth Stetson and LuAnn St. Johns.

Communications = Partay.

(Laughing. Not laughing.)

I seem to have lost the skill set at some point.

Then I met Jonafer's father and the rest is all downhill... I mean...history.

THE REST IS HISTORY!

It has been great. Fantastic. Really. I don't know why I...

Why I said that.

I love my kids.

(To Jonathan.) I love you Jonathan.

I mean – you could be like ten thousand times less picky about food, but other than that – no complaints.

Where was I?

Oh. Yes.

I love my kids.

I love my job.

Being a MOM!

> *(Looking at card.)*

Okay. Right.

I am a mom!

CAREER DAY! MOM!!

I bet you didn't know that being a mom was a career?

Well – I mean – I guess technically it isn't a career – as it were.

But – I mean – it is a job.

It's just one of those jobs where you work really hard and don't get any credit and no one notices you and if a *man* did the same job they would get a ton more money – so – yes.

Yes. It is like any other job that a woman would get.

That sounds...

That sounded.

Bad.

I – it is VERY fulfilling *(Is it?)*

It is.

I swear.

Being a career mom is – well – it isn't everything I ever wanted but it – well...

Close.

> *(Looking at Ms. Cohen.)*

This is getting off track.

> *(Looking at card.)*

I wrote a list of things that I do:

> *(Reading.)*

Wake up Jonathan.

Wake up Jennifer.

Wake up Sam.

Cook breakfast.

Make lunches for everyone.

Serve breakfast.

Call everyone down for breakfast.

Shoot myself because this sounds so boring.

No. No.

I mean, I am very happy, I am, but come on –

this isn't intellectually stimulating or creative or I don't know.

(Silence.)

I thought I wanted to be an actress.

A star, I guess.

Yes.

I wanted to be on stages and screens and magazines.

I wanted to light up a room with my – with my "magnetism" – no "magneticism."

Like the greats.

Judy Garland!

Marlene Dietrich!

Barbara Stanwyck.

I know you don't know these people – but – trust me…

THEY *WERE*… *(Searching.)* LIT. Lit?

Oh gosh.

I used to imagine myself center stage – singing…

Like… Like…

(It has just come to her.)

Carol Channing.

Oh god. Yes! Carol.

Carol Channing.

Hello Dolly!

(She is losing herself in the story.)

She was in the very first play I saw. You know what a play is?

Hello Dolly!

It was a touring production in St. Petersburg, Florida.
They called it BROADWAY IN THE SUNSHINE!
My mother dropped me off – because we could only
afford one ticket. I remember getting my program,
sitting in my seat and pouring over the details.
The curtain rising.
The band playing.
The actors and singers.
The dancers.
It was magical.
I was transported.
To…
Astoria or Yonkers – no – Astoria.
I don't know.
It was fantastic. So great. So funny.
I love that moment.
When she's like…

    (Now in a brilliant Carol Channing accent:)

"Horace Vandergelder you go your way…
…and I'll go mine."

    (She does the action of pointing her hand in
    one direction and then instead of pointing in
    a different direction – she points in the same
    direction.)

"You go your way and I will go mine."

    (Back to herself.)

I just loved that moment.
But there was – so much – it was so… Amazing.
Like how you all must feel seeing Beyoncé or – I don't
know – Run-hana – whoever that is?
And then – when she did the big – the big number –
"Hello Dolly."
She appeared at the top of this grand staircase.
Wearing this long – elegant – divine – gown.

And feathers. Feathers in her hair. FEATHERS!
Practically floating down the stairs...and singing...
She was singing.

> *(She opens her mouth, she is sooooo in the moment, right there again, and she really really wants to belt out the song.)*
>
> *(But.)*
>
> *(She can't sing.)*

Well, Hello...
OH GOD.
I can't sing.
IMAGINE me singing!

> *(She starts to "dance" around the stage and semi-lip-synch, but it looks a bit odd. Perhaps it looks very odd but she is lost in the moment. Then she remembers and snaps back to* **SALLY**.*)*

Oh. Yes. Then she starts to walk the – what do you call it – the thingy – that ramp around the orchestra? The...

> *(Back to Carol.)*

The passerelle! Yes. The passerelle.

> *(Back to* **SALLY**.*)*

And she starts to walk the passarelle and sing.
Then when she gets to the very middle.
Practically standing amongst us.
She STOPS.
The music STOPS.
She looks out at us all.
She has us eating out of the palm of her hand and she says,

> *(Back to Carol.)*

"I LOVE YOU ST. PETERSBURG."

(*Back to* **SALLY**.)

(*In a whisper.*) I love you St. Petersburg.

(*Silence.*)

(*Silence.*)

Now. I had several feelings.

One.

I was in heaven loving it.

Two.

I didn't understand why the character of Dolly Levi was speaking to the people of St. Petersburg when the play is clearly set in Astoria. Or Staten Island. Somewhere – not St. Petersburg, Florida

But it didnt matter. I was hooked.

I wanted to do *that*.

(*Back to Carol.*)

I love you St. Petersburg!

(*Change.*)

But – there is a point here.

The point is. The point is that.

Well.

Touring productions in Florida might not have been the highest quality.

No.

No. My point is that.

I swear I have one Ms. Cohen.

Careers.

Yes!

So – I started taking dance classes and doing plays and musicals.

I even wanted to be a theatre major in college and I played Sally Bowles in *Cabaret*.

(*She hits a "Sally Bowles" pose with a showbiz/jazz hands noise like "huzzah."*)

I loved it when the mirror came down at the end of the show.

Implicating the audience – in – well – you'll learn about meta-theatricality later.

Oh Gosh. I could have been. I could *be* Carol Channing – here today – talking to you – telling you about traveling the country – stopping in the middle of songs on passerelles and making little girls dream about big big things.

Things that might have been too big to dream about.

But.

Well.

Life happened.

And I met Sam.

And I – well – he got a job. San Francisco.

And I – had Jennifer.

And.

I love my life – I do – I really do.

I love you Jonathan.

And I am proud to be – a – a mom.

I am very proud.

I am.

   (Beat.)

Yes!

That's what I wanted to say to you all for Career Day.

   (Beat.)

Give up on your dreams!

No.

That's not.

No!

Have a dream!

Yes. You should have dreams.

But – know – that sometimes – sometimes

those dreams can change.

They can morph into new dreams.

Dreams you never imagined for yourself.

And then at some point you'll be hanging a painting that your child drew for you,

or watching a video of your daughter's ballet recital

or speaking at your son's Career Day and you realize –

you realize...

That you are incredibly...

Just incredibly –

Happy.

　　(Silence.)

Damn. Career Fairs make me horny.

　　(Blackout.)

End of Play

Printed in the USA
CPSIA information can be obtained
at www.ICGtesting.com
JSHW011253061224
74946JS00004B/187

9 780573 708459